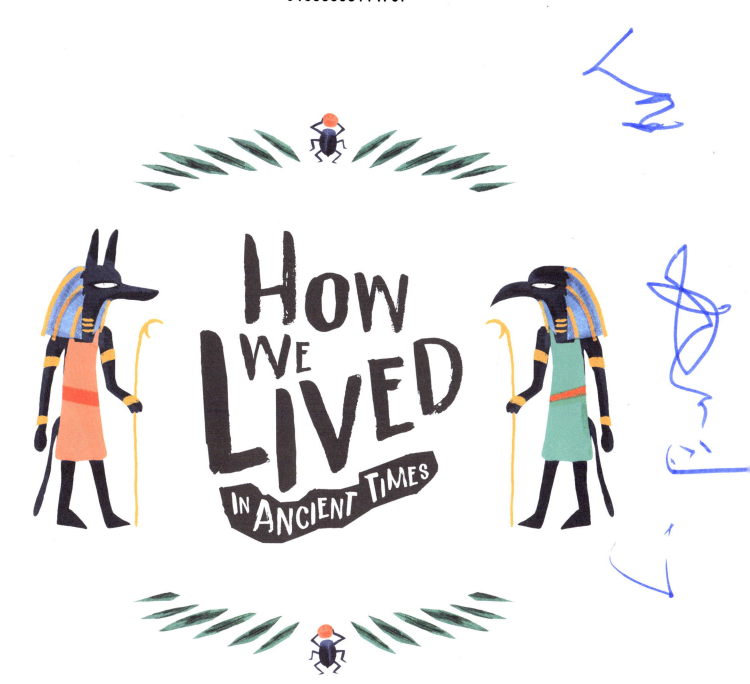

HOW WE LIVED IN ANCIENT TIMES

WELBECK

Published in 2021 by Welbeck Children's Books

An Imprint of Welbeck Children's Limited,
part of Welbeck Publishing Group
20 Mortimer Street London W1T 3JW

Text and design © Welbeck Children's Limited,
part of Welbeck Publishing Group.
Illustrations © Christiane Engel

A CIP catalogue record for this book
is available from the British Library.

ISBN 978 1 78312 703 0

Printed in Heshan, China

10 9 8 7 6 5 4 3 2 1

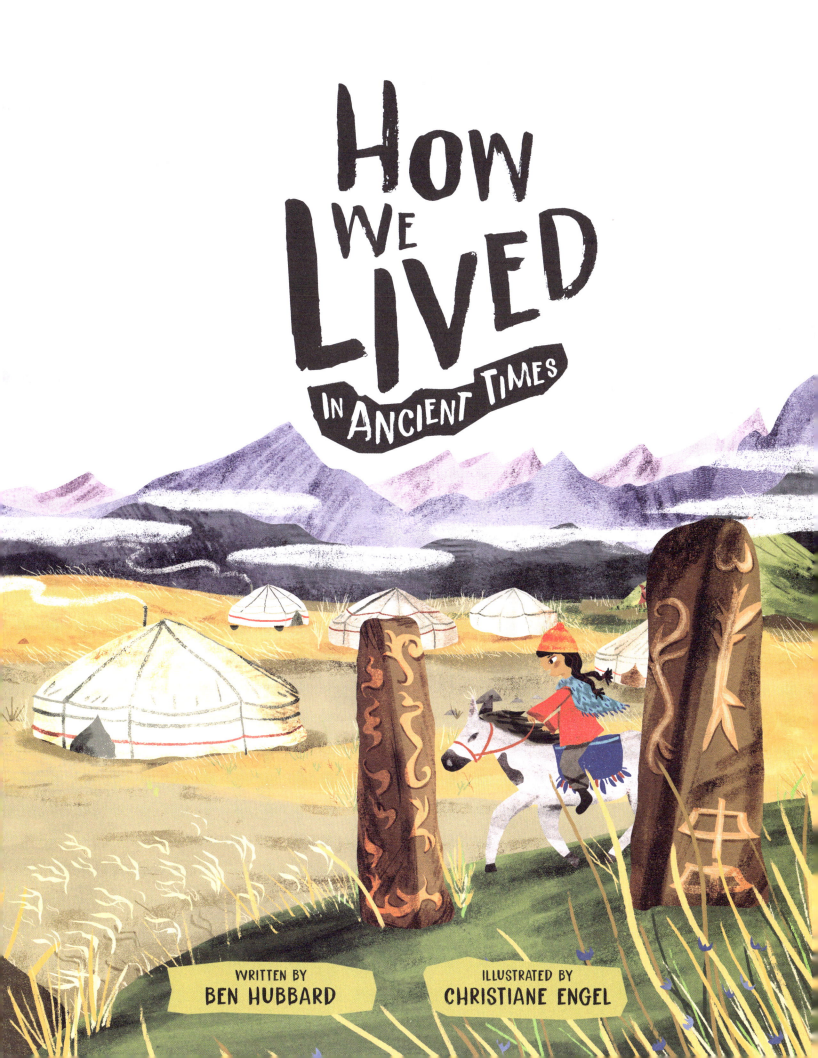

How We Lived
in Ancient Times

WRITTEN BY
BEN HUBBARD

ILLUSTRATED BY
CHRISTIANE ENGEL

Imagine if you were born in the Stone Age... or in Ancient Egyptian times,
or as a Roman or Viking. Your life might have been very different.
It might have been more dangerous, more exciting, and perhaps even more fun!

Hello! I am Mat, and my family never stays in one place for long!

I'm Itza, and I live in a city with no streets!

I am Hanish. Want to climb to the top of the temple with me?

Welcome! My name is Ara. Let's join the pharaoh's procession!

The children in this book are from cultures across ancient history.
They want to show you how they ate, played, worked and lived.
So come on in – they can't wait to meet you!

I'm Ki! Ever seen a giant stone head? I can show you one.

Hey! I bet you can't ride a horse as fast as me, Argim!

Nice to meet you! I'm Selene, and my lighthouse has incredible views.

Good morning! I am Suiko. Let's explore the emperor's court.

Greetings! I am Freya, and it's time for a warrior's feast!

TIMELINE

HANDY MAN

3.3 million years ago – 1.9 million years ago

One of our earliest human ancestors was *Homo habilis* ('handy man') from Africa. *Homo habilis* could walk on two legs and make stone tools to hunt with. Meat and bone marrow from the hunts helped *Homo habilis's* brain evolve.

HUNTERS AND GATHERERS

40,000 BCE – 10,000 BCE

By 40,000 BCE, modern humans had populated many parts of the world. They lived in groups and moved from place to place to find food. These hunters and gatherers survived by killing animals and foraging for food, such as berries and nuts.

See Paleolithic on pages 8-13.

THE FIRST CITIES

8,000 BCE – 3,000 BCE

From 10,000 BCE, farming settlements in western Asia grew into the first cities, made of mud brick and stone. The city people soon had their own cultures, and worshipped different gods. They traded with their neighbours and made artworks from clay, wood and bone.

EARLY HUMANS

1.9 million years ago – 300,000 years ago

Over time, Homo habilis evolved into *Homo erectus* ('upright man'). *Homo erectus* could make fire and stone hand axes, and eventually left Africa to live in Asia and beyond. *Homo erectus* evolved into *Homo sapiens sapiens* – modern humans.

THE FIRST FARMERS

10,000 BCE – 8,000 BCE

Around 10,000 BCE, many parts of the world became warmer. Neolithic-era people domesticated animals, developed tools to grow crops and set up the first farms. This allowed people to settle in one place.

See Neolithic on pages 14-19.

ANCIENT CIVILISATIONS

3,000 BCE – 1,200 CE

From 3,000 BCE, cities in Egypt, China and Mesopotamia grew into the world's first civilisations. Ruled over by kings, priests and emperors, the civilisations built large temples, palaces and tombs, and protected their borders with armies.

See Sumer on pages 20-25.

See Ancient Egypt on pages 26-31.

See Olmec on pages 32-37.

GREAT EMPIRES

500 BCE – 500 CE

During this time, powerful civilisations called empires invaded large areas of land and ruled over the conquered people. Over half the world's population lived in three major empires: the Roman in Europe, the Han in China and the Parthian in western Asia.

See Alexandria on pages 44-49.

THE MIDDLE AGES

1,000 CE – 1,500 CE

The Middle Ages in Europe began with barbarian invasions and ended with journeys of discovery by great explorers. Elsewhere, the African Bantu kingdom was founded, the Incas formed South America's largest empire, and Polynesians discovered New Zealand. The modern world followed.

THE AGE OF IRON

1,200 BCE – 100 BCE

From around 1,000 BCE, iron replaced bronze as the main metal used in tools and weapons. Advances in farming and a growth spurt in the world's population followed. As iron became easier to get hold of, more people had weapons, leading to more wars.

See Scythians on pages 38-43.

THE DARK AGES

500 CE – 1,000 CE

By 500 CE, the large empires of the ancient world had fallen and new empires in Japan and central America emerged. Religions including Christianity, Islam and Buddhism spread. There were large migrations of people displaced by the fallen empires.

See Japan on pages 50-55.

See Vikings on pages 56-61.

PALEOLITHIC

YEAR: 15,000 BCE
CULTURE: Hunters and gatherers
LOCATION: France

UPPER PALEOLITHIC
The Upper Paleolithic Period began around 40,000 years ago and ended 10,000 years ago.

SYMBOL FIGURES
The Lascaux Cave contains over 600 paintings and 1,500 engravings of animals and symbols.

EXTINCT AUROCHS
Some of the paintings are of animals now extinct, such as the aurochs bull.

Hello! I am Mat, daughter of Po. Welcome to the Lascaux Cave. Please come inside and see some of the world's first cave paintings.

My tribe doesn't live in this cave all year round, but we shelter here for the coldest winter months. We are hunters and gatherers. This means we move from place to place. We forage for food, such as berries and nuts, and hunt animals for their meat. We depend on animals for our survival. That's why we make cave paintings of them. Come and see, but be careful not to bump your head. it's dark in here!

From around 40,000 BCE, people lived in many parts of the world. This time is known as the Upper Paleolithic Period, which means 'Old Stone Age'. These people dressed in animal furs, used stone tools and hunted large animals for food. They also created sculptures and wall paintings. The Lascaux Cave contains some famous examples. They were made around 17,000 years ago.

Dordogne, France

Woolly Clothes

We make our own clothes from animal skins and furs. The best animals for making clothes are bison, reindeer and woolly mammoths. After eating the flesh of these animals, we cut off their skin and leave them to dry in the air. We then sew the skins into clothes using reindeer-bone needles. Do you like my dress? It's brand new!

ODD ONE OUT
There are no paintings of reindeer in the Lascaux Cave, even though it was common at the time. Nobody knows why!

SIMPLE SYMBOLS
The Lascaux Cave paintings and engravings include dots, lines and rectangular symbols.

Ibex Lamp

Our cave is long, dark and deep. It has several passages and chambers and the sunlight can't reach inside. So we light small fires in the centre of some chambers and also use flaming torches and lamps to see. This lamp is made from limestone and has patterns carved into the handle. We burn animal fat in the lamp.

Mammoth Sculpture

As well as cave paintings, small sculptures and figurines were carved from stone, wood and bone. These sculptures often showed common animals of the time, like reindeer. This bone sculpture shows two reindeer swimming through a river.

Hand Axe

This stone hand axe could chop wood, scrape animal skin and cut meat. Often made from flint or volcanic rock, hand axes were chipped into a sharp edge with another, larger stone. The first axes were made by early humans around 1.2 million years ago.

Spear Thrower

Woolly mammoths were large elephant-like mammals that were hunted by Upper Paleolithic people. It would take a group of men wielding spears to bring one mammoth down. A spear thrower, which was attached to the end of the spear, gave a hunter more throwing power.

Foraging Food

Animal flesh was the main source of food for Upper Paleolithic people. But they also foraged for berries, roots and nuts to eat. The people would stay in one place until there was no more food, and then move on. It was not until around 10,000 BCE that hunters and gatherers began settling in one place to grow crops and farm animals.

BIRDS AND CATS
The Lascaux Cave animal paintings include seven big cats, a bird, a bear and one human.

Sharp Points

During the Upper Paleolithic period, bones, tusks and antlers. These were made into tools like arrow heads, spear points, harpoons and fishhooks. Often these sharp instruments were made with rows of barbs to stop them being pulled out by wounded prey.

THE LASCAUX CAVE PAINTINGS

The Lascaux Cave paintings show which animals were most common during the Upper Paleolithic period. The paintings show deer, horses, bulls, bison, ibex, lions, bears and even a rhinoceros. These animals were carefully painted in colours of brown, yellow, black and red. The colours were created from pigments found in local plants and the earth. The paintings were created in many different sizes, some no bigger than a hand. The largest painting, of an aurochs bull, is over five metres long.

The artists used the bumps of the cave walls to make their animals look three-dimensional.

The pigment was made into a powder and water added to make paint.

Scaffolds and ladders were needed to reach higher sections of the cave.

Hollowed-out bones were used to blow paint onto the figures.

NEOLITHIC

YEAR: 6,500 BCE
CULTURE: Çatalhöyük
LOCATION: Turkey

I'm Itza! Welcome to Çatalhöyük, one of the world's first cities. We are so glad you can join us in our unique community!

Our city has no streets or walkways, just houses built tightly next to one another, back-to-back. Our houses have no windows or doors, but instead have small holes in the roof to get in and out. Outside, the roofs are like our streets and communal spaces rolled into one. We may be an ancient people, but we have very modern ideas! We know the importance of keeping clean and understand that men and women are equal. We also dedicate a lot of time to creating useful objects and beautiful artworks. Come down into my home and I'll show you some of them!

FAR RANGING
Instead of roaming like their ancestors, the city people farmed the land around them.

HIGH LIFE
Cooking, cleaning, meeting and playing all took place on the rooftops of the city.

BURIED BELOW
The bones of ancestors were buried directly underneath the rooms of the living.

People first started building this amazing mud-brick 'city' around 7,400 BCE. Hundreds of years earlier, hunters and gatherers had abandoned their nomadic lifestyle to settle on Turkey's fertile Konya plain and farm. Later, they decided to try urban living. The result was a place famous for its architecture and artworks. Between 3500 and 8000 people lived in Çatalhöyük.

Europe

Çatalhöyük

Modern-day Turkey

Asia

Africa

Marvel at our Map

During your stay, make sure to check out our map of the area. This shows the city itself and the nearby mountain where we mine our obsidian. The mountain is actually a volcano, which erupted many years ago. Don't worry though — people say it's no longer active.

Plentiful Food

People have farmed here for many years. We keep sheep and goats, and grow our own vegetables and grains. Don't forget to try our delicious bread! The countryside gives us apples, almonds and pistachio nuts and we hunt bison, deer, boars and birds. Here, we are all equal so men and women share exactly the same food.

Burial Bed

In each Çatalhöyük home, several raised platforms were used for sleeping and relaxing. They were covered with animal skin. The platforms would even be used as burial mounds for the bodies of dead relatives.

Wall Paintings

The inside walls of Çatalhöyük's homes were covered in white plaster and decorated with black and red paintings of human hands, animals and patterns. Leopards, boars, bears and wild bulls were all depicted. Painted scenes included people pulling their tails and tongues and jumping on their backs.

Bull-horn Decoration

Wild bulls were holy in Çatalhöyük. Their plastered skulls were used to decorate the walls and platforms in people's homes. The pointed horns of these skulls would be left pointing out and sometimes painted ochre red.

DEATH BELOW
Dead relatives were buried right below sleeping areas. Imagine trying to sleep over your ancestor's bones!

Flint Dagger

Because the people of Çatalhöyük grew their own crops and farmed animals, they had time to craft useful objects. Bone and flint were used to create tools and weapons. They even made mirrors with volcanic glass called obsidian. Flint daggers, such as this one, had decorative bone handles.

Goddess Figurine

The Goddess Figurine is a small, seated female statue flanked by leopards on either side. The statue was found in one of the granaries of Çatalhöyük, where it was probably intended to protect the grain supply. Many other statues of people and animals were discovered in the city's remains.

ÇATALHÖYÜK HOME

Inside each house, there were no windows. Instead of a door, people used a ladder to go in and out through a hole in the ceiling. Below the ladder was an oven. The floor around the oven was blackened with soot and ash and covered with reed mats. Raised platforms built above the floor were used as the house's clean spaces. Cleanliness was important in Çatalhöyük: homes were kept swept and tidy and rubbish was burned. For this reason, people in Çatalhöyük were healthy and lived long lives for their time.

Ladder to the roof

Wall paintings over white plaster walls

Oven

Bull horn decoration

Door to storeroom

Basket

Raised platform

Broom

Animal skins

19

SUMER

YEAR: 2800 BCE

CULTURE: The Sumerians

LOCATION: Mesopotamia

Nice to meet you! I am Hanish, son of Humbaba, a Sumerian scribe in our city-state of Ur.

Ur is one of the first cities in the world. It is built around a giant temple called a ziggurat and surrounded by a high, stone wall. Inside the city, there are houses, granaries, assembly halls and palaces. Our lugul, or king, protects us with his army and makes sure we are all well fed. Most people in Ur work for the lugul or the priests. The temple employs lots of craftsmen, labourers and scribes. My father is one of these scribes. Come into the city and I'll show you around.

PRAY PROCESSION
Many people pray and make offerings to the gods at the ziggurat's shrine.

FEEDING FARMLAND
Irrigated farmland around Ur provides its people with food.

CITY KILNS
Potters make the mud bricks the city is constructed from in their kilns.

The Sumerians were the ancient people of Mesopotamia, modern day Iraq, who built some of the world's first cities around 4,000 BCE. These cities thrived because of new irrigation techniques that enabled year-round agriculture. This provided a surplus of grain which was stored and used to feed the city's large workforce. The Sumerians were not a united people, but instead made up of city-states such as Ur and Uruk. Each city-state was governed by laws and a king and at their peak were inhabited by up to 50,000 people.

Sumer

Persian Gulf

Middle East

TIGRIS TRADE

Ur was an important trade city because it was situated where the Tigris and Euphrates rivers ran into the Persian Gulf.

GILGAMESH

The adventures of a famous Sumerian king called Gilgamesh were described in an ancient poem, the Epic of Gilgamesh, which was written on clay tablets.

Sumer School

Not everyone can afford to go to school, but I am one of the lucky ones. At school I am learning how to be a scribe, just like my dad. Scribes are highly regarded in Ur and a good scribe is never out of work. Sumerian school are strict — if you misbehave then the teacher canes you!

Sumer Game

I hope you've been enjoying your tour of Ur. But the city is not all about hard work. How about a round or two of our favourite board game, Twenty Squares? It's one of the oldest board games in the world and it's played as far away as India and Egypt. It uses counters and pyramid-shaped dice.

Cuneiform Tablet

The Sumerians invented the first type of written language, called Cuneiform. Cuneiform was made up of symbols and signs and was inscribed into wet, clay tablets with a reed pen. The tablets were then baked in a kiln to make them hard.

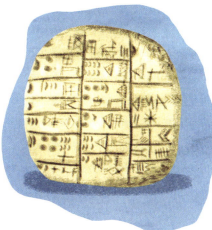

Bevel-rimmed Bowl

The workers in Ur were very well organised. Some of the workers laboured in the fields and harvested grain. The grain was stored in the city's granaries and paid out to the workers. Each worker had a special clay bowl to collect their wages.

Standard of Ur

The people of Ur made magnificent objects from lapis lazuli, shells and marble from the Middle East and India. The Standard of Ur is a lavishly decorated box showing scenes of the city's lugul. In one scene, the lugul is accepting offerings; in another, he is trampling his enemies underfoot.

City Soldiers

The lugul of Ur employed an army to protect the city and attack his enemies. Sometimes a Sumerian city-state conquered another, but no ruler united the whole of Sumer. A typical Sumerian soldier wore a thick cloak and copper helmet and fought with a spear, sling and bow and arrow.

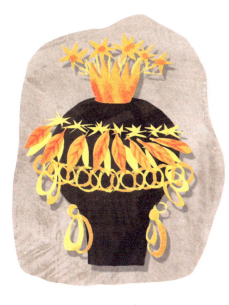

Royal Headdress

The royals of Ur wore the finest clothes and jewels and were treated like gods. This headdress made of gold and precious stones once belonged to Ur's Queen Puabi. It was buried with the queen in around 2,550 BCE.

RIVER DESERT
Ur was founded in 4,000 BCE and lasted until 400 BCE, when the Euphrates River changed course and the farmland turned into desert.

ZIGGURAT

Ur's ziggurat was the city's most important temple. It was a three-storied, stepped building made from mud bricks and surrounded by ramps and stairs. Great religious processions would climb the stairs of the ziggurat to the shrine at the top, where priests would perform elaborate rituals and ceremonies. Ordinary workers would leave small clay statues of themselves as offerings to the gods. The priests were important people in Ur and second only to the royal family. The priests were not only religious leaders, but also employed large numbers of workers and craftsmen to make textiles and other items.

Ur's ziggurat was over 30 metres high.

The shrine was dedicated to the moon god Nanna, the protector of Ur.

The temple staff lived and worked in small houses, workshops and offices outside the ziggurat.

The staircases converged at a great, central gatehouse.

Three great staircases over 100 steps high led to the upper shrine.

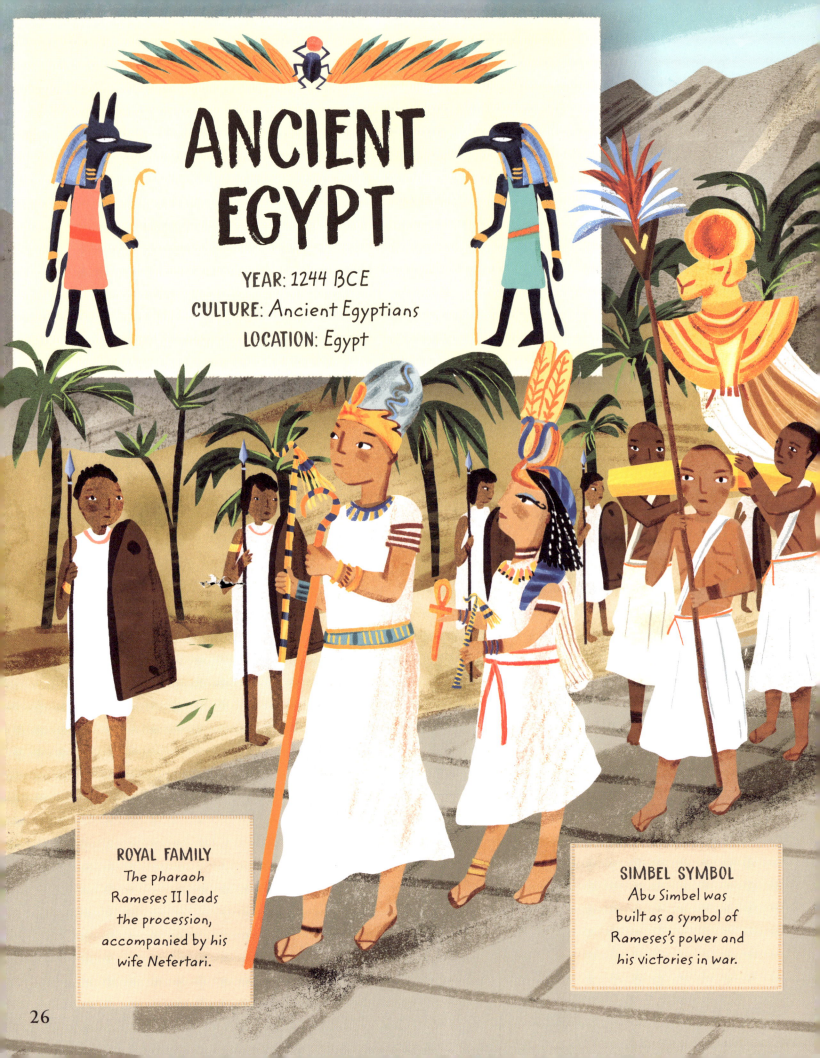

ANCIENT EGYPT

YEAR: 1244 BCE
CULTURE: Ancient Egyptians
LOCATION: Egypt

ROYAL FAMILY
The pharaoh Rameses II leads the procession, accompanied by his wife Nefertari.

SIMBEL SYMBOL
Abu Simbel was built as a symbol of Rameses's power and his victories in war.

RAMESES TWICE
Two 20 metre high statues of Rameses sat on either side of the temple entrance.

Welcome to Egypt! My name is Ara, daughter of Sebi, a labourer and stonecarver.

Shhh! This is a very grand occasion. It's the opening of my dad's latest project, a new temple called Abu Simbel. The temple is carved into a cliff face with four massive statues at the front. The statues are of Rameses II, our beloved pharaoh. Rameses and his wife, Queen Nefertari, are attending the opening ceremony, which is held by the temple priests. After the ceremony there will be a banquet with music and dancing. We Egyptians know how to party!

The Ancient Egyptian civilisation began along the banks of the River Nile, North Africa, around 7,000 years ago. Egypt developed into a formidable single kingdom ruled over by powerful pharaohs. The pharaohs would order the construction of pyramids, temples and statues in their honour and wage war with their enemies. Ancient Egypt is remembered for its magnificent tomb paintings and artworks, its massive building works and its elaborate religion and belief in the afterlife.

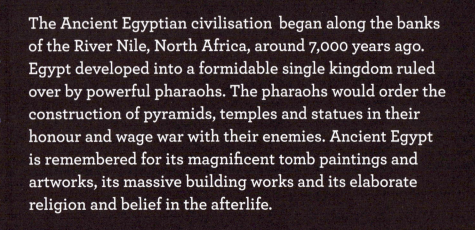

Egypt

EYE MAKEUP
Egyptians took a lot of pride over their appearance, with both men and women wearing eye makeup.

The Flooding Nile

After visiting Abu Simbel, take a stroll with me down to the River Nile. Ancient Egypt is a dry, desert-like place and we need the waters of the Nile to survive. Every year, the Nile floods, which leaves behind a layer of silt that makes the fields fertile. We then plant our crops of wheat, barley and vegetables. We store the grain and barley left over from our harvest in large granaries, for when there is less food.

CATS AND CROCS
Animals such as cats and crocodiles were mummified as offerings to the gods.

Ships and Sailboats

Do you like sailboats? Lots of Egyptian children have a toy sailboat to play with. Mine is built like the boats that travel up and down the Nile. We use boats to transport people and goods, and giant blocks of stone to building sites. Temple boats are used to carry statues of gods and goddesses during religious festivals. The royal navy also has its own fleet of warships!

Writing Hieroglyphs

The Egyptians developed a system of writing called hieroglyphs. Hieroglyphs were made up of around 6,000 picture symbols that described objects, ideas and sounds. Scribes were trained to write hieroglyphs from the age of nine. Hieroglyphs would appear on tablets, temple walls and papyrus, a type of paper.

Tomb Paintings

A pharaoh's tomb was believed to be their home for all eternity, so more care was taken to construct and decorate it than the palaces they left behind. The walls of a royal tomb were painted with scenes from everyday life, the gods, and the pharaoh's journey to the afterlife.

Pharaonic Jewellery

Egyptian bracelets, armbands and rings were designed to not only look beautiful but ward off evil, bring good luck and please the gods. Some of the most magnificent Egyptian jewellery was buried with a pharaoh, such as Pharaoh Tutankhamen's death mask.

The Gods

Egyptian gods and goddesses were shown with animal heads and headdresses in tomb paintings and were often known by several different names. The Sun God was called Ra and the pharaohs were believed to be his sons.

Mummification

The Egyptians believed that death was not the end, but simply the start of their journey to the afterlife. Here, their body and spirit would be reunited. For this reason, the Egyptians carefully preserved a person's dead body with salts and resin, then wrap it in bandages. These Egyptian 'mummies' have survived for thousands of years until the present day.

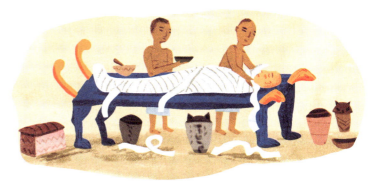

THE GREAT PYRAMID

Rameses II built the temple of Abu Simbel in 1244 BCE. But over 1,200 years earlier, Egypt's most famous building was constructed: the Great Pyramid. Made as a tomb for Pharaoh Khufu, the Great Pyramid is the largest stone building ever constructed and a marvel of ancient engineering. Khufu began construction on the Great Pyramid as soon as he came to power in 2575 BCE. It took over 20,000 men working day and night for 20 years to complete the pyramid. This meant a giant stone block weighing as much as an elephant was put in place every few minutes! The Great Pyramid contained over 2.3 million stone blocks and was clad in smooth, white limestone. In 2566 BCE, Khufu was laid to rest in a chamber in the heart of the pyramid.

Workers on the pyramid were not slaves — they were paid and also offered a place in the afterlife with Pharaoh Khufu for their contribution.

Teams of between 5 and 20 workers used sledges, tree-trunk rollers, ropes and levers to pull the largest blocks.

Workers included quarry workers (who dug out the stone), hauliers (who pulled the giant stone blocks into place) and stonemasons (who cut each stone into shape).

Every team had 20 workers, each with a project leader and specific task.

Once in place, copper chisels and mallets were used to cut the stone blocks into the correct shape.

OLMEC

YEAR: 800 BCE
CULTURE: The Olmecs
LOCATION: Mexico

RUBBER PEOPLE
Olmec means "people of the rubber country" in the Mayan language.

Hello stranger! We are pleased you can join us in La Venta, the great city of the Olmecs. I am Ki, son of Bada.

We Olmecs were the first people to set up a civilisation in Central America. We invented many things that were later copied by the Mayans and Aztecs. Pyramid-shaped temples, the chocolate drink, worshipping jaguar gods and a ritual ballgame played with the first ever rubber ball – they all came from us! But perhaps the Olmecs are most famous for our colossal heads, carved from massive blocks of stone. Can you see one behind me?

GODLY OFFERINGS
Many offerings were made to the gods at La Venta, including statues and sculptures.

PYRAMID PINNACLE
La Venta featured the largest Mesoamerican pyramid of its time.

33

The Olmec civilisation began as clusters of villages in south-central Mexico. Fertile growing conditions and plenty of fish from the rivers allowed the populations to grow. From around 1200 BCE, the Olmec cities of La Venta and San Lorenzo emerged. The cities were ruled over by an elite, who oversaw a workforce of fishermen, farmers, traders and artisans. The artisans were responsible for great artworks and sculptures made from stone and jade.

Modern-day Mexico

Olmec range

NEW WORLD WRITING

In around 650 BCE, the Olmecs produced one of the first writing systems in the Americas.

Olmec Ball Game

One of the must-see attractions for visitors is our ball game. Make sure not to miss the next match! The game is played by four to six players with a hard ball made from solid rubber. The aim of the game is to keep the ball off the ground and through one of the hoops in the wall. But the players cannot use their hands or feet. The hard ball is heavy, so causes many bruises. Ouch!

Rubber Tapping

My dad is one of the city's best rubber tappers and it's fun to watch him work. To make rubber we extract latex – a milky sap – from trees. We do this by making a cut and then collecting the leaking latex. The latex is then mixed with juice from the vines of the morning glory plant to make rubber. This rubber is then fashioned into a ball.

Drinking Chocolate

The cacao bean was one of the crops grown by the Olmecs, alongside corn, squash, sweet potatoes and tomatoes. The cacao bean was fermented and mixed with water to make drinking chocolate, containing honey, red chilli, cinnamon and vanilla.

Jade Mask

The Olmecs carved stone and jade masks to represent their rulers and dead ancestors. This jade mask may have been worn as a death mask by a dead king or priest.

MESOAMERICAN FOLLOWERS
The Mayan and Aztec peoples who followed the Olmecs had a similar culture and beliefs.

Step Pyramid

At the centre of La Venta was a 30 metre-high stepped pyramid with a shrine at its top. The city's other buildings included a palace, a ballcourt, several tombs and a large plaza where public gatherings were held. Olmec buildings were made from clay and not built to last.

NO GOODBYE
The Olmecs mysteriously disappeared in around 100 BCE. No-one is sure what happened...

Cave Paintings

The Olmecs created colourful cave paintings in red, brown and blue. This painting shows an Olmec ruler next to a standing jaguar. The 'were-jaguar' was one of six gods the Olmecs worshipped. The others included a Shark Monster, a Feathered Serpent and an Olmec Dragon!

Infant Sculpture

Many Olmec sculptures were of babies, either holding a ball or being held by an Olmec ruler. Some of the babies are 'were-jaguar' infants, because they are shown with fangs and slanted cat eyes. Other babies are shown with a cleft in their mouths, the Olmec symbol for corn.

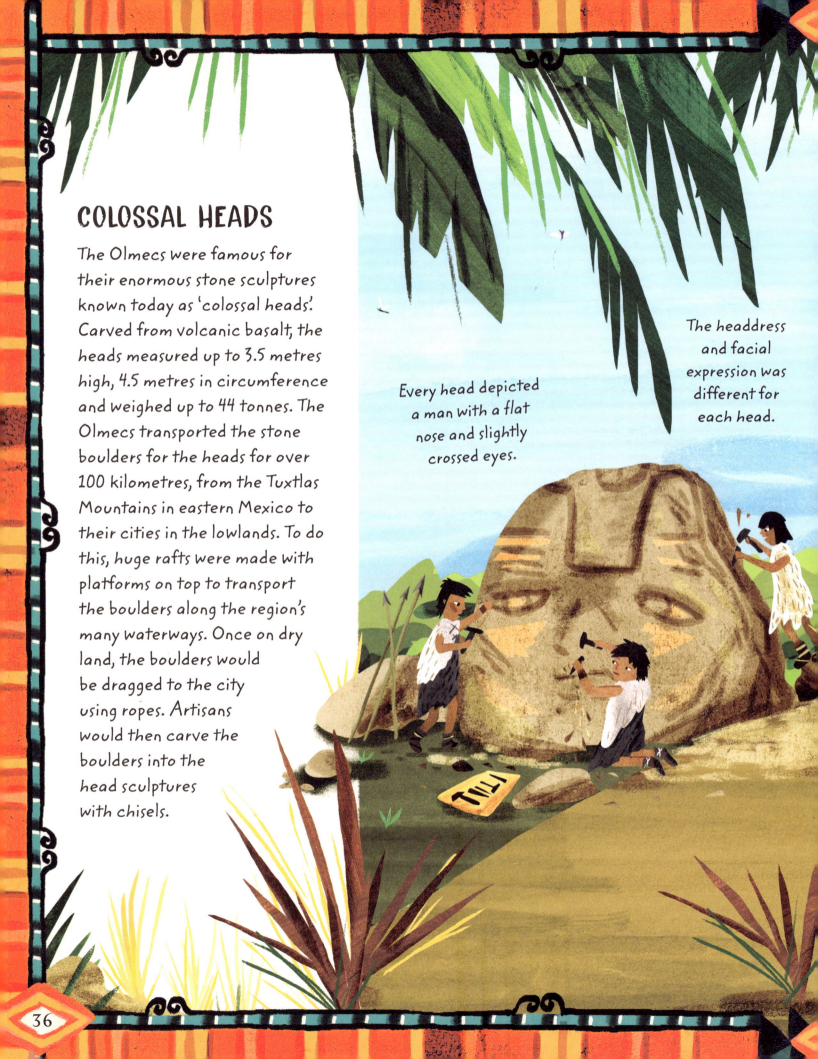

COLOSSAL HEADS

The Olmecs were famous for their enormous stone sculptures known today as 'colossal heads'. Carved from volcanic basalt, the heads measured up to 3.5 metres high, 4.5 metres in circumference and weighed up to 44 tonnes. The Olmecs transported the stone boulders for the heads for over 100 kilometres, from the Tuxtlas Mountains in eastern Mexico to their cities in the lowlands. To do this, huge rafts were made with platforms on top to transport the boulders along the region's many waterways. Once on dry land, the boulders would be dragged to the city using ropes. Artisans would then carve the boulders into the head sculptures with chisels.

Every head depicted a man with a flat nose and slightly crossed eyes.

The headdress and facial expression was different for each head.

Each head
represented a
different ruler.

The heads were
either arranged in
lines or groups, or
positioned alone.

Some of the
stone heads were
buried in special
chambers, perhaps
as an offering.

SCYTHIANS

YEAR: 700 BCE
CULTURE: The Scythians
LOCATION: Eurasian Steppe

Welcome to the wide, wild plains of the Scythians.
I am Argim, daughter of the horseman and warrior Oguz.

We Scythians live in the grassy region known as the Eurasian Steppe. Here, we ride horses, herd animals and move from place to place in our covered wagons. We are also formidable warriors who are both feared and admired for fighting from horseback. Can you ride a horse? Jump on the back of mine and I'll show you around.

HERODOTUS HISTORY
Much of what we know about the Scythians was written by Greek historian Herodotus in the 5th Century BCE.

POWERFUL PERSIANS
The Scythians were powerful enough to stop an invasion by the mighty Persian king Darius in 513 BCE.

BLOOD DRINKERS?
Some accounts say that Scythian warriors used to drink the blood of their defeated enemies.

Originating in Iran, the Scythians conquered the Eurasian Steppe and founded an empire that stretched from Eastern Europe, across Siberia to the borders of China. The Scythians, however, did not unite under one ruler except in times of war. Instead, they were made up of a federation of nomadic tribes. These tribes moved from place to place in the Eurasian Steppe, where they reared horses and built elaborate burial mounds. From the 2nd Century BCE, the Scythians faded from view.

Eurasian Steppe

HEAD COUNT

Scythian warriors counted the number of enemies killed in battle by collecting their heads.

Feasting

Today we are having funeral feast for one of our fallen warriors. It is a sad day, but also a celebration of their life. Please join us as there will be plenty to eat. We eat lots of butter, milk and cheese but our specialty is boiled meat. We throw everything into the pot, meat and bones, and then serve it up as a stew. Delicious!

GREEK GOLD

Some Scythian gold jewellery was made for them by ancient Greek craftsmen.

Drink Up

Everything we Scythians own is small, lightweight and can easily be carried from one place to another. For this reason, we all have our own cups. Did you bring one? Scythians love drinking wine and fermented alcoholic milk. We also drink normal goat's milk. Here, use my cup to try some!

Mounted Archers

Scythian archers fired from horseback and struck terror into the hearts of their enemies. Able to ride quickly into the most effective position, banks of archers would shower an enemy force with hundreds of arrows in only a few minutes. Some Scythian archers were said to dip their arrows in poison.

Jewellery

Scythian jewellery included bracelets, necklaces and brooches which often depicted animal scenes. On this belt ornament, a big cat is shown mauling a horse. Other pieces of jewellery show mythological creatures, such as the griffin, which had the body of a lion and the head of an eagle.

DOUBLE BOW
The Scythians were eventually replaced by the Sarmatians, who had a similar culture.

Battle Axe

When not firing a bow and arrow, the Scythians would fight with a battle axe called a sagaris. It had a metal head that was often sharp at one end and blunt on the other. The head of a sagaris was mounted onto a long, wooden shaft so it could be wielded from horseback.

Burials

Deceased Scythian warriors and nobles were laid to rest in large burial mounds. Their horses and worldly possessions were buried with them. But first, their bodies were mummified. This involved stuffing the bodies with dried grass and sewing up the skin. Mummification kept the bodies intact for hundreds of years.

Tattoos

Male and female Scythians were heavily tattooed with patterns, animals or mythological creatures. A tattoo discovered on a 2,500-year-old mummified Scythian princess show a deer with a griffin's beak and long, elaborate antlers.

HORSEMAN

Horses were essential to the Scythian way of life. The Scythians initially bred herds of horses for their milk and hides. But later, the Scythians became the first people in the world to harness and ride horses. To do this, they developed the saddle, an invention which was then copied across the known world. It meant they could mount attacks on their enemies at 50-60 kilometres per hour. A horse was a warrior's prized companion. Scythian horses would be dressed in ceremonial outfits with colourful saddles and decorative headgear. Dozens of horse skeletons have been found alongside the bodies of chieftains in Scythian burial mounds.

Tail with plaits and ribbons

Soft, warm cap

Long-sleeved tunic

Belts with weapons attached

Ornamental belt buckle

Decorative headgear

Colourful saddle cloth

Quilted trousers

43

ALEXANDRIA

YEAR: 150 CE

CULTURE: Romans, Greeks, Egyptians

LOCATION: Egypt

Good day! Please join me for the best view of the greatest city of the ancient world. I am Selene, daughter of Lathyros, Alexandria's lighthouse keeper.

When day turns to dusk, my dad lights the beacons of Pharos, the tallest lighthouse of the ancient world. But during the day, it's a great place to look out over the magnificence of Alexandria. Built in northern Egypt by Alexander the Great, Alexandria is today ruled by the Romans. It's made up of many different nationalities and cultures. It is also a hotbed of learning – many great minds from around the world have lived, worked and studied here. Come with me and I'll show you my city.

CAMPAIGN CITY
Alexander founded over 70 new cities during his 10 year conquest of Europe, Africa, the Middle East and Asia Minor.

ROME VS ALEXANDRIA
In the ancient world, the only city bigger than Alexandria was Rome.

CITY OF GRAIN
One story says that Alexander drew out his plans for Alexandria in grain.

The Macedonian king Alexander the Great founded Alexandria in 332 BCE. Many of the city's buildings, including the Pharos Lighthouse and Library, were the largest of their kind. Great thinkers moved to Alexandria, which was taken over by the Romans under ruler Augustus. The city continued to be Roman until the 4th century CE, when Alexandria became a Christian city and many of its pagan-era buildings, including its library, were destroyed.

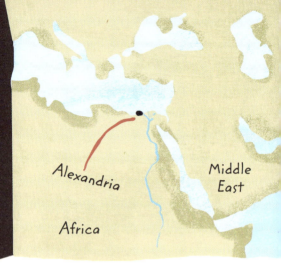

Alexandria

Africa

Middle East

How are you enjoying the amazing city of Alexandria? Come with me and we'll explore the agora, or city square. The agora is a feature of every Greek city and is a great place for people to meet. It is surrounded by colonnades, statutes and shops. There's often a market in the agora too, which sells everything from olive oil, to slaves, to figs – just the thing for an afternoon snack!

Alexander's tomb

Alexander the Great founded Alexandria as a vital trading city between east and west. Although he was Macedonian, he had been schooled in Greek traditions. So Alexandria was built in the Greek style. Alexander was buried in Alexandria when he died in 323 BCE.

JEWISH HOME
Alexandria was home to one of the largest Jewish communities of the ancient world.

The Serapeum

The Serapeum was a Greek temple built in the 3rd century BCE and dedicated to the Greco-Egyptian god, Serapis. Serapis was worshipped as a Sun god, like the Egyptian god Ra. One of the largest Greek temples in the east, the Serapeum was constructed with great marble columns and a large inner platform on which the statue of Serapis sat.

Cleopatra's Needle

Obelisks were large, Egyptian stone columns inscribed with hieroglyphs. Cleopatra's needle was a 21-metre-high obelisk originally constructed in 1475 BCE. In 12 BCE, the obelisk was moved to Alexandria in honour of the Roman general Mark-Antony and Cleopatra, the last pharaoh of Egypt.

Nileometer

Alexander's general Ptolemy had to construct a series of underground channels to bring the waters of the River Nile into the city. However, once a year the river flooded. To warn of this, Ptolemy used a traditional Egyptian nilometer. This showed when the river was rising, so they could block the water with dams.

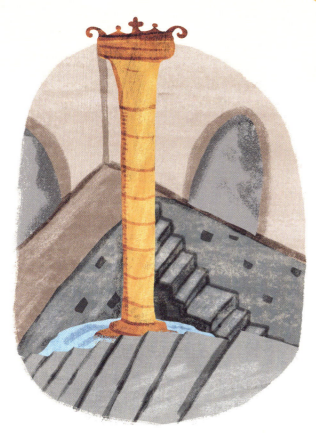

CONTINUING CAPITAL
Alexandria was the capital of Egypt until 642 CE, when it was invaded by Arab forces.

The Lighthouse

At around 120 metres high, the Pharos lighthouse was one of the tallest structures constructed, and one of the Seven Wonders of the Ancient World. Built from large blocks of stone, the lighthouse had a circular section at the top in which a fire was built. The light from the fire was then reflected out to sea using large bronze mirrors.

Trading City

Alexandria became one of the great trading cities of the ancient world. The goods that were exported from Alexandria included glass, grain, medicine, perfume and jewellery. Imported into Alexandria were elephants from Somalia, gold from Nubia, copper from Cyprus and silver from Spain.

VICEROY DYNASTY
Alexander's general Ptolemy went on to found the dynasty which bore his name.

THE LIBRARY

Alexandria was created as a centre for learning and at its heart was the largest library the world had known. The library contained over 49,000 books from places all over the ancient world. The library even hired people to seek out new texts that it didn't have. There were books on maths, science and medicine and some of the best-known scholars and philosophers, such as Euclid, Archimedes and Plotinus, moved to Alexandria. One scholar named Hero of Alexandria made many inventions at the library, including the syringe and an early steam engine. Another scholar, Herophilus, made the discovery in Alexandria's library that the human heart pumped out blood around the body. Despite books coming from all around the known world, most of the texts in the library were written in Greek.

The books in the library were mostly written on papyrus scrolls called bibliothekai.

The library was fitted with Greek columns throughout.

The library at Alexandria included study rooms, laboratories, botanical gardens and an observatory.

HEIAN JAPAN

YEAR: 800 CE
CULTURE: Japanese
LOCATION: Japan

DIVINE RULER
The emperor was considered the divine ruler of Japan. But by the end of the Heian period he had lost his power.

Good morning and welcome to Heian-kyō, the capital city of Japan. My name is Suiko, daughter of Fujiwara no Musashi, a commander, poet and nobleman of the imperial court.

You've chosen an interesting time to visit, as Japan is undergoing a period of great change. At the imperial court, Japanese culture is blossoming. Everyone wants to move to Heian-kyō to be part of it. The court nobles are known as the *kuge*. Their lives are filled with court ceremonies, religious rituals, dances, games and poetry competitions. As a young *kuge* girl, I have to watch from the corner. Not fair!

SŌHEI WARRIORS
Buddhism was the main religion of Japan. As its influence grew, so did the emergence of Sōhei: Japanese warrior monks.

The Heian Period from 794-1185 CE is known as the Golden Age of Japan. Before then, Japan had borrowed many of its ideas from China. But from the 8th century, Japanese art, architecture, literature, religion and rituals flourished, especially at the imperial court. However, the emperor's control began to weaken during this time. Taking control would be a Shōgun, a military leader who commanded a powerful samurai army.

Heian-kyō

Japan

DAIMYO SHŌGUN
The most powerful daimyo could become the military ruler of Japan, called the Shōgun.

Courtly Beauty

We women have to stay in the background at the court, but are also expected to look beautiful. We paint our necks and faces with a thick, white powder. We also shave off our eyebrows and paint them high on our foreheads. We paint our lips bright red and wear our hair long. We then blacken our teeth, so they don't look yellow next to our white skin.

Kemari Football

Life at court never gets boring. Make sure to check out a game of kemari while you're here. A little bit like football, the game is played by two teams who use their feet to kick a ball. However, there are no winners or losers in kemari. Instead, the object of the game is simply to pass the ball to the other players. Hmm, maybe this does get a bit boring after a while!

Bugaku dances

These ceremonial dances were made up of slow, minimal movements performed to increasingly fast music. The dancers often wore wooden masks with exaggerated facial expressions. This is because at the court, real facial expressions were considered rude!

RITUAL SUICIDE
If defeated in battle or dishonoured, samurai warriors would commit ritual suicide, called seppuku.

Byōdō-in

The Byōdō-in was built in 998 CE as a villa for the Fujiwara clan, but became a Buddhist temple in 1052 CE. Then, a new 'Phoenix Hall' was constructed at the Byōdō-in to house a new 2.4-metre statue of Buddha.

Class System

During the Heian period, the emperor became increasingly dependent on powerful warlords, known as daimyos. Daimyos were the rulers of clans who were sworn to protect their emperor from barbarians. The clans were made up of warriors called the samurai.

Rice Paddies

While the emperor and nobles enjoyed life at the imperial court, Japanese peasants toiled in the fields to feed them. The emperor, the temples and court nobles all owned land in Japan. But the Fujiwara nobles at the imperial court did not have to pay taxes. This made them very rich.

EMISHI BARBARIANS
The Emishi were the native people of northern Honshu, Japan's main island. The imperial court considered them barbarians.

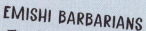

Literature

During the Heian period, noble men and women were both taught to write and produce poems or stories. One of the Heian period's most famous novels was written by a woman, Murasaki Shikibu Nikki. Murasaki's *The Tale of Genji* was a love story about a fictional prince, Genji.

JAPANESE KNIGHTS

The Samurai were Japanese warriors originally charged with protecting the emperor's borders from the Emishi 'barbarians'. Samurai lived to a strict honour code called Bushido, the 'Way of the Warrior'. Bushido demanded honour, loyalty and fearlessness in war. Those who broke the Bushido code were even expected to kill themselves! In battle, samurai warriors would issue challenges to each other before engaging in one-to-one combat. This would begin with a mounted archery duel and end on the ground with swords drawn. The winner of the bout would be honour-bound to cut off the loser's head.

There were hundreds of styles of samurai helmets, called Kabutos.

Samurai armour had to be light enough to shoot a bow, but strong enough to survive a sword blow.

A samurai's katana, or sword, was his prized possession.

Heian period armour was called Yoroi, or 'great armour' and had a box shape.

Samurais also carried a smaller sword, called a wakizashi.

Samurai armour was made from lacquered leather plates that were laced together.

VIKINGS

YEAR: 900 CE
CULTURE: Vikings
LOCATION: Norway

Greetings! I am Freya, daughter of Svein, a farmer and Viking warrior.

We Vikings are great explorers and often travel to foreign shores in our longships. There is not much land to farm at home, so when we sail to a settlement abroad we either raid, trade, or invade – depending on our needs! Today, a party of warriors is returning after raiding along the coast of England. Vikings do have a reputation as ferocious warriors, but we are not savages. Our villages are civilised places where we spend time with family, tend our animals, and create beautiful objects from metal and bone.

WEAPONS PRACTICE
Viking warriors had to practice their skills with sword, spear and bow.

BEWARE THE BESERKER!
Berserkers were dangerous warriors that even scared other vikings.

RETURNING SHIPS
The shallow-bottomed Viking ships can sail far up-river for raids.

The Vikings were the seafaring people of Norway, Sweden and Denmark who came to prominence in the late 700s. For nearly 300 years, Viking warriors terrorized the communities of Europe by attacking monasteries, raiding settlements and launching entire invasions. The Vikings also set up vast trade routes that stretched from Ireland to Istanbul and settled in many European countries and beyond.

Sweden

Norway

Denmark

Food

Today, preparations are being made for a feast to celebrate our warriors' return. We will be eating hot bread, fish, mutton, goat, salted pork, carrots, peas, turnips and fresh berries. The food will be washed down with mead made from honey and beer.

GRITTED TEETH
Viking bread often contained grit from the grinding stone, which broke people's teeth!

Gods

We Vikings believe in many gods who are ruled over by Odin, the creator of humans. Thor, the god of thunder and lightning, is my favourite. Thor causes the sky to crack as he rides across it in a chariot pulled by two goats. He wields a mighty hammer called Mjöllnir. We believe the world will end in the mighty battle between the gods and giants called Ragnarok.

Mjöllnir

Olof

Berserkers

Watch out for Olof the berserker during your stay. Berserkers are our fiercest warriors, who enter a state of rage called 'berserkergang' before battle. During berserkergang, warriors bite their shields, froth at the mouth and fight with a crazed frenzy that terrifies our foes! However, when not at war berserkers make trouble around the village. Please don't get into a fight with Olof, even if he provokes you!

Longships

Viking longships were swift, sleek and built with a shallow bottom to land on beaches or travel up rivers. Powered by both sails and oars, longships were perfect for ambushing unsuspecting settlements.

Jewellery

The Vikings were master craftsmen who made intricate jewellery from silver, gold, bronze and bone in their workshops. Vikings wore finger, neck and arm rings, as well as necklaces and pendants.

Weaponry

A Viking's weapons were his prized possessions and he would be buried with them after death. Warriors carried spears, axes and swords and protected themselves with helmets, chainmail shirts and wooden shields.

SPLIT SILVER
When abroad, silver Viking jewellery was often taken off, cut up and used as currency.

SWORDS AND SPOONS
Viking women were buried with their kitchen utensils in the same way men were buried with their weapons!

Games

The Vikings held outdoor competitions including archery and spear-throwing, but also enjoyed indoor games, such as gambling with dice. Hnefatafl was a board game found in many Viking settlements. It was played on a checkered board with two sets of pieces, a bit like chess.

Longhouses

Viking families lived in homes called longhouses, which were dark, smelly and smoky places. One end of the longhouse would act as a barn for animals and crop storage, while a fire in the middle would provide heat and light. Benches around the walls were for relaxing and sleeping.

A KING'S BURIAL

Vikings were often buried with their treasure when they died. Weapons were a Viking warrior's most prized possessions. Vikings fought with swords, axes, spears and bows and arrows. Swords were expensive and treated as precious family heirlooms, passed down from father to son. The most famous swords had names such as 'WAR FLAME,' 'LIFE TAKER' and 'LEG BITER'. A warrior would need their weapons in the afterlife, called Valhalla. This was a great hall ruled over by the king of the gods, Odin. Viking warriors who had died in battle would live in Valhalla for eternity. They would spend their days fighting and their nights feasting and drinking. Most Vikings were buried in simple burial mounds, but kings and nobles were sometimes laid to rest in their longships, which were then covered with soil.

IN THE SHIP TOMB

* A powerful Viking king
* Necklaces and bracelets
* Gaming board with horn counters
* Fish hooks and fishing line
* 30 swords, axes and spears
* 64 shields
* Kitchen utensils
* 1 sleigh
* 3 small boats
* 6 beds
* 12 horses
* 8 dogs
* 2 peacocks

GLOSSARY

Agora - In ancient Greece, a public open space used for markets and other meetings.

Artisan - A skilled worker who makes useful or beautiful things.

Aztecs – the people who lived in Mesoamerica in the 13th century. They were fierce warriors who built a strong empire that lasted for more than a hundred years.

Cuneiform – the written language of the ancient Sumerians. They used a wedge-shaped tool made from a reed to press marks and symbols into wet clay.

Eurasian Steppe – an area of grassland that extends from Hungary and across Asia for about 8,000 km.

Hieroglyphs – the written language of the ancient Egyptians. 'Hieroglyphs' means 'sacred signs'. Each picture symbol represented a word, an idea or a sound.

Incas – the people who lived in western South America during the 15th century and early 16th century. They built a huge and successful empire that dominated the area during this period.

Irrigation – the supply of water to agricultural land to help crops grow.

Mayans (or Maya) – the people who lived in Mesoamerica from 1000 BCE until 1697 CE. They shared the same religion and culture, but each city within the region ruled itself.

Mesoamerica – the region of Mexico and Central America occupied by the Aztecs, Mayans and other cultures like the Olmecs and Incas.

Mesopotamia – the area between the Tigris and Euphrates rivers in what is now Iraq. The name is Greek and means 'land between the rivers'. Mesopotamia is the birthplace of the world's first civilisations.

The Middle Ages – the period of history in Europe from 500 CE after the collapse of the Roman Empire to 1500 CE. Also known as the Medieval period.

Mummification – the process, called embalming, in which dead bodies were preserved by drying them out and covering them in layers of linen wrapping.

Neolithic – a period of the Stone Age, which began about 10,000 years ago, when people started farming crops and animals. The word 'neolithic' is Greek meaning 'new' (neo) and 'stone' (lithic).

Nilometer – a device used to measure the water levels in the River Nile.

Nomadic – moving around a lot. A nomad is a person who moves from place to place, in search of food and land to graze their animals.

Obelisk – a four-sided pillar made of stone that becomes narrower towards the top and ends in a small pyramid-shaped point.

Observatory – a building or place used to observe or study the planets, stars and space, and weather and other natural phenomena.

Obsidian – a black volcanic glass, formed when lava cools rapidly.

Olmec – an ancient people living in south-central Mexico from about 1200 BCE to about 400 BCE. They were the first civilisation of this area. The word 'Olmec' means 'rubber people' from the rubber trees in the area.

Paleolithic Period – the earliest period of the Stone Age, from about 2.6 million years ago, when early humans first started making stone tools.

Papyrus – a material like paper made from reeds, and used by ancient peoples to write on.

Pharaoh – a ruler of ancient Egypt. The pharaoh was the political and religious leader and was thought of as a god. Pharaoh comes from a word meaning 'great house'.

Prehistory – describes the time before people invented writing.

Scribe – a person whose job was to make written copies of documents.

Scythians – an ancient nomadic people, who were famous for their horse-riding skills, and who dominated the grasslands of the Eurasian Steppe.

Seven Wonders of the Ancient World – a list of seven great buildings or structures from ancient civilisations. The most commonly known list is The Great Pyramid of Giza, the Hanging Gardens of Babylon, the Statue of Zeus at Olympia, the Temple of Artemis, the Mausoleum of Mausolus, the Colossus of Rhodes and the Pharos Lighthouse of Alexandria.

Shōgun – a military title meaning 'General' in Japanese. In ancient times in Japan, the Shogun were the top generals in an emperor's army. The Shogun became the rulers of Japan from the 13th century until late in the 19th century.

Stone Age – the time when early humans used tools and weapons made out of stone. It is divided into the Paleolithic, Mesolithic and Neolithic – the old, middle and new Stone Age.

Ziggurat – an ancient Mesopotamian temple, constructed in a pyramid-shaped structure built on many levels.

INDEX